Akhtaruzzaman Elias:
Beyond The Lived Time of Nationhood

Series Editors

Pratyush Chandra

Ravi Kumar

Radical Notes 1

Akhtaruzzaman Elias:
Beyond The Lived Time of Nationhood

Pothik Ghosh

AAKAR

AKHTARUZZAMAN ELIAS:
Beyond The Lived Time of Nationhood
Pothik Ghosh

First Published, 2008

ISBN 978-81-89833-50-3

Published by
AAKAR BOOKS
28 E Pocket IV, Mayur Vihar Phase I, Delhi-110 091
Phone : 011-2279 5505 Telefax : 011-2279 5641
aakarbooks@gmail.com; www.aakarbooks.com

Printed at
Mudrak, 30 A Patparganj, Delhi-110 091

A movement in a sense is a struggle over the definition of reality—how reality is constituted. It is this struggle that builds the focus and targets of the movement, informing the praxes towards social transformation. Inherent in this struggle is the act of reclaiming—sense and sensibility, words and meaning...

The word "radical", which in this post-Cold War phase of Global Capitalism or globaloney has been reduced to a general notion characterizing all kinds of extremism and deviance, is one such word that has been time and again reclaimed by the practitioners of social transformation. "Radical" derived from the Latin word, 'radix' meaning 'root' = 'basic' = 'fundamental' is a concept that aptly defines a transformatory practice as an endeavour to reveal and target the essence of what is given to us in appearance. Radicalism in this sense is nothing but fundamental transformation rather than politicking in appearances. Further, and foremost, it is the all-round critique of the status quo and its genealogies, rather than accepting the disciplinary divide/boundaries that the capitalist system perpetuates in order to control labour-power and labour, our efforts and their fruits.

Radical Notes is an endeavour to coordinate the radical voices around the globe, with special focus on South Asia. In our view such focus (which could have been anything) is not just for convenience, given the facilitators' cultural and intellectual comfort, but is also needed to concretise any 'radical' pursuit. In our view South Asia provides us the opportunity to visualize the reproduction of 'global' capitalism and struggle against it in a regional setting. But we must remember such focus is always fluid with the ever-dynamic radical needs of the humanity.

Radical Notes booklets are contributions on social, cultural, political or economic issues from counter-hegemonic perspectives, which need not be confined to any established socialist and communist current of thought (though these approaches are most welcome).

Series Editors
Radical Notes

And to say now that you are no longer here is to say only that you have entered a different order of things, in that the one we move in here, we latecomers, as insane as it is, seems to our way of thinking the only one in which "god" can spread out all of his possibilities, become known and recognized within the framework of an assumption whose significance we do not understand.

— From **Eugenio Montale's** 'Visit to Fadin'

Introduction

If there is a time for everything, there must be a time for revolution too. But revolutionary time can often become its own time warp. It can freeze one moment, among many, of revolutionary politics into its eternalised truth and thus prevent such politics from recognising the new moments of revolutionary reality that lie beyond the moment it has mystified as its be-all. Concomitantly, such mystification also prevents it from realizing its own potential. This potential can be sensed and expressed only when revolutionary politics is driven by the will to relentlessly transcend its various moments to constantly encounter itself within different possible historical temporalities. Alas, it is the South Asian Left more than any other, either in the 'Third' or 'First' World, that has been the worst victim of this historical time freeze. A self-containing, even psychotic, numbness, which goes by the name of national anti-colonial resistance, has held South Asian 'revolutionary' praxis in its tightly malignant grip for the past five decades. The upshot: it still articulates its politics in terms of nation—preponderantly, in the idiom of national sovereignty and independence.

Clearly, its understanding of revolutionary politics continues to be haunted by the spectres of its origins, which lie in a 'third world' conjunctural complex of national-liberation struggles against direct colonialism on one hand and 'socialist' struggles against neo-colonialism on the other. The failure of the South Asian Left, particularly its Indian strand, to posit its politics shorn of all idioms of national independence, and in classical Marxist terms of class struggle per se, must be ascribed to its cussed refusal to acknowledge the fact that imperialism as a phenomenon has long outgrown its colonial (or neocolonial) moment of oppressive politico-economic occupation of foreign lands.

It is in this context that Bangladeshi writer Akhtaruzzaman Elias's politico-aesthetic framework, especially the way he expounded it through his novels *Khowabnama* (Dream Chronicle) and *Chilekotar Sepai* (The Soldier in the Attic), acquires immense importance. The praxis of cultural politics that this framework adumbrates would, if adopted by the South Asian Left, open up new pathways of resistance and revolution beyond the confines of its stale and stifling national-liberation paradigm. The attempt here is to envisage the politico-aesthetic vision of the Bangladeshi author, together with that of filmmaker Ritwik Ghatak's, as an integral part of an exiguous though crucial ideological strain within what may provisionally be called the Bengali Left. The fundamental politico-aesthetic impulse of Elias and Ghatak's art, and their stance on the political in general, could be constitutive of a new politics of resistance that is free from the vicissitudes of the national-liberation paradigm.

PARADIGMS OF REVOLUTION OR PRISONS OF REACTION

We will truly appreciate the pressing need for such a praxis when we fully reckon with the incalculable damage South Asian Left's near complete dependence on idioms of national independence/sovereignty has done to its struggle against imperialism. Its reliance on this outdated paradigm to understand, critique and intervene in the current politico-economic situation has prevented it from coming to grips with the new moment of "imperialism without colonies".

That has not only rendered the Left here incapable of formulating its anti-imperialist struggle — now more a shibboleth than a critical vision of politics — as anti-capitalism, it has also sapped our comrades of all capacity to accurately diagnose the reason behind the degeneration of the originally progressive national-liberation projects of their respective societies into jingoistic authoritarianisms and/or reactionary fascisms. It would do its purported politics of anti-imperialism a whole load of good if the Left were to accept the fact that we are now part of a decentred empire of various nationally deterritorialised capitals competing with one another. Its inadequate and ineffectual response to the rising tide of fascisms and various other forms of reactionary identity politics in this part of the world must, to complete the dialectic of haplessness, be blamed on its stubborn persistence with the timeworn frameworks and categories of national liberation.

Much of its supposed critique of fascism, as a result, is embedded in and imbued by categories of bourgeois ethics and liberal modernity, which prove ineffective precisely because it fails to zero in on the political-economic essence or logic of fascism. Fascism has to be located as a problem of the larger socio-economic structure, of which liberal modernity, bourgeois ethics of secularism and imperialism are constitutive elements. For instance, the Indian Left's programmatic attempt to pose 'secular' and 'economic' nationalism against, simultaneously, the 'cultural nationalism' of RSS-BJP-type fascist forces and 'western' imperialism shows it is completely oblivious of the political economy of the nation-state. Such nationalistic anti-imperialism has not only weakend its struggle against the national component of global-imperialist capital, it has not in any essential sense enabled the Left to critique fascism because it shares with the fascists, particularly of the Hindutva variety, the same structural and logical premises (nation, nationalism, national pride etc) of politics. All that the various strains of the Indian Left have done so far by way of resisting the Hindutva forces is load those categories with a superficially different ethical or normative charge. Not surprisingly, all those leftist strains have without exception been condemned to fight fascism on the latter's terms and turf. They have, we have, failed grievously to posit any structural alternative to the current political-economic order that fosters fascism and imperialism as dialectical halves of one single phenomenon: "globalisation".

ELIAS AND GHATAK: NEW AND DIFFERENT PATHWAYS

It is in the backdrop of globalisation that the significance of Elias and Ghatak's conceptions of art, aesthetics and politics must be fully unravelled and grasped. Both the writer and the filmmaker, separated by almost a generation and national boundaries, were critical of the national-liberation paradigm, particularly in the context of Bangladesh's struggle for independence.

They both recognized, and depicted through their art, the obfuscatory and obstructionist nature of that paradigm, vis-à-vis the essential project of social revolution. Yet, more important and interesting than this similarity of their critiques is the difference in their politico-aesthetic register and orientation. Elias's critique of the national liberation/nationhood paradigm is, thanks to this difference, more fundamentally anti-systemic. There is absolutely no doubt that the social revolutionary aspirations of the urban underclass, poor peasantry and radical intelligentsia of Bengali East Pakistan — against the expropriative and exploitative machinations of the West Pakistani elite, its Rawalpindi-based military executive and their local agents — was the trigger of the national liberation struggle that erupted with the "Bhasha Andolan" (language movement) of 1952. Elias has shown as much in *Sepai*. But what is equally true is that linguistic-cultural (Bengali) nationalism was, in terms of this elemental social revolutionary impulse, a unifying local ideological idiom of resistance. Especially since West Pakistani colonialism played itself out in East Pakistan in Punjabi racist and anti-Bengali terms. Considering that this colonialism — a local extractive moment of the global political economy of imperialist capital — was held together in the name of a Muslim national brotherhood by a ruling class consisting of West Pakistanis and a sizeable chunk of East Bengalis, this idiom of Bengali nationalism was, to begin with, useful. Ultimately, however, Bengali chauvinism subsumed and subverted the fundamental social revolutionary impulse of the national-liberation struggle of Bangladesh. A fact noted and critically depicted by both Ghatak and Elias in their cinema and literature respectively.

In Ghatak's last film, *Jukti Takko Gappo* (Logic Argument Story), protagonist Neelkantha, Ghatak's alter ego, deliberately severs himself from the general sense of nostalgia for a united Bengal rampant among the petty-bourgeois intellectuals of Calcutta-centric Indian West Bengal. What may seem surprising is that Ghatak/Neelkantha — despite his exilic yearning for a lost idyll and the concomitant dream of a West Bengal reconciled with east — does not share the petty-bourgeois optimism in vogue in contemporary West Bengal about the power of the linguistic-nationalist liberation struggle to achieve real reconciliation.

In fact, he violently rejects such optimism. His rejection embodies not only the impossibility of the fulfilment of this fantasy, but also its undesirability. This sensibility is, in a certain sense, classically Marxian as its expression is at one and the same time ethical and political. For Neelkantha (and Ghatak), the unity of Bengal is not merely about the overcoming of a superficial religious (Hindu-Muslim) divide to reconcile a linguistically-culturally 'similar' people. It is also about accentuating the various inflection points between reified 'conventional' and elitist (bhadralok) Bengali culture and various 'little' cultures dotting the Bengal-Bihar-Orissa continuum.

It is Ghatak's conception of a more dialogic, organic and composite Bengaliness that drives him, through Neelkantha, to accentuate those inflection points. But such Bengaliness is only a cultural epiphenomenon of something much more essential. The premise of Ghatak's vision, in contrast to the petty-bourgeois culturalist perspective of 'one Bengal', is political-economic. Ghatak seeks to underscore the reification of modern Bengaliness and, in the process, points out the political-economic logic of production of territorialised and stratified cultural differences. It must, however, be mentioned that Ghatak's vision is informed as much by his encounter with a Marxist critique of capitalist political economy as it is rooted in the non-Renaissance cultural sensibility of Bengal. This sensibility of Atish Dipankar (a 10th-11th century Buddhist monk from Bengal) and Chaitanya, who pre-date the so-called Bengal Renaissance, was borne forward by figures such as Ramakrishna Paramahansa and even partially Rabindranath Tagore during the Renaissance. (It must be stated as an aside that Tagore, contrary to his conventional image, was not a full-fledged Renaissance hat. He was split between the romantic individualism and realism of Renaissance and a self-effacing classicism specific to various communitarianisms in pre-modern Bengal.) Renaissance privileged the modern, knowing subject situated within a telelogically fraught romantic gaze, and thus established the supremacy of knowledge objectified, captured and represented by this gaze. In so doing, it created the fundamental terrritorialised hierarchy between the knowing culture (on top) and the known culture (below it) and served to destroy the composite organicity of pre-Renaissance communities, what with genteel 'Bengaliness' emerging as an alienated, superordinate, and determining centre, vis-à-vis the various 'little' and 'demotic' cultures around it.

But the grounding of Ghatak's critical political-economic prism in a communitarian cultural sensibility leads, not surprisingly, to its contamination. As a result, communitarian organicity does not function merely as logic of negative dialectical critique of alienation and the political economy of capitalism. Instead, it is envisaged as a lost and transcendental Arcadia. As a result, Ghatak's rejection of culturalist euphoria over the "impending" reconciliation of Bengal ends up denying the sedimented class reality immanent in the Bangladeshi war of national-liberation.

And this is exactly where Elias's political, and aesthetic, approach becomes distinguishable from Ghatak's. Growing up in East Pakistan, the writer has to confront the question of national liberation much more directly. So, while he shares Ghatak's critique of the obfuscatory idiom of national-liberation, once it became the predominant ideological form of articulating resistance in East Pakistan, he does not stop looking for possibilities of social revolution immanent in this form. In *Chilekotar Sepai*, he dwells at length on how the children and grand-children of elite Muslim Leaguers among the local, Bengali-speaking East Pakistani population gradually seized the leadership of the liberation struggle as they saw the tide turn. It also shows how this seizure of leadership was accompanied by an excessive emphasis on Bengali linguistic unity against the Urdu-speaking colonialists of Pakistan, even as the fundamental socio-economic question of the peasantry and working class was first relegated to the background and subsequently suppressed. Such precedence of nationalist Bengali unity over socio-economic transformation served to conceal and repress a very crucial aspect of Pakistani colonialism in East Bengal: the exploitation and oppression of the East Bengali working class and peasantry by the local elite, patronized and protected by Rawalpindi. But the most insightful aspect of the novel, as far as we are concerned, is the legitimacy the Communist Left of East Bengal conferred on this turn of events by slowing down and then withdrawing from the peasant struggles against landlordism in countryside. But this understanding of Elias, which accurately highlights the perils of confronting colonialism as a cultural-linguistic phenomenon, does not force him to reject the Bangladeshi national liberation struggle in its entirety. Unlike Ghatak, he seeks to foreground the possibilities of social revolution immanent in and repressed by a struggle that has come to be seen as a pure cultural-linguistic movement. The character of underclass Haddi Khijir, whom Elias creates as a counterpoint to Marxist intellectual Anwar and other more cynical upholders of Bengali nationhood — like Khijir's employer Allaudin, nephew and son-in-law of loyal Muslim Leaguer Rahmatullah — is meant to simultaneously emphasise this possibility and its repression.

What foregrounds Elias's search for immanent possibilities of social revolution in the Bangladeshi national-liberation struggle is the last section of *Sepai*, where protagonist Osman Gani, till then an inert inhabitant of the oppressive status quo, locates through his delirious visions the drive, strength and truth of the national-liberation movement in the upsurge of the urban underclass and lumpen-proletariat of East Bengal. That Khijir, shot dead by the Pakistani army, should come to life in Osman's dreams and hallucinations to become a beacon of the national-liberation movement precisely at the moment when the crucial social revolutionary impetus of the liberation struggle is being contained in the name of Bengali linguistic-national unity bears Elias's concerns out. The moment when Osman's delusions force him to deny and withdraw from existential reality and its rationality is as much the moment of his insanity as the point where he acquires a different historical individuality than the one he had till then embodied. This transformation happens through his realignment, albeit delusively, with a new political practice and formation that resists the socially exploitative and politically oppressive reality of existential time. Madness becomes the science of revolution.

Frantz Fanon's assertion that a national-liberation struggle is nothing if it does not become a struggle for social emancipation is, it seems, also Elias's credo. Anti-colonialism is a cry against forcible extraction of surplus value before it's a demand for national-political self-determination. In fact, the search for such self-determination is simultaneously political and socio-economic. Clearly, the question of political power cannot be dealt with in isolation from the question of socio-economic relations. The logic that underlies the creation of a differential hierarchy of identities, whereby the colonizing identity determines the destiny (and identity) of the colonized, is the logic of the exchange value-driven political economy of capitalism. It is a logic, which through competition and/or coercion, introduces alienation into a horizontal, non-identitarian flow to produce a differential of political power and/or socio-economic entitlements and thus creates a vertical stratification of *different* identities.

Such focus on the socio-economic logic of both colonialism and anti-colonialism is important because representative democracies, particularly in ex-colonies such as ours, have a way of obscuring this essence by projecting liberation from foreign rule as the end of the search for self-determination. It seems to suggest that colonialist abominations consist entirely of how colonizers go about their business, and not what that business is. They have, in their representation of colonialism, falsely privileged the use of coercive force by our former colonizers over what that force was actually meant to achieve: transfer of value from a certain section of people, who were compelled to give up control over their means of production, to those who took possession of those means either directly or by setting the rules of the market. Such obfuscation, largely structural, is also sometimes wrought through voluntaristic and deliberate propaganda. It is meant to conceal the fact that a change in the form of government does not change the essential political-economic logic or the class character of the state, which continues to play its crucial role of aiding value transfer for capital accumulation. Liberal representative democracy is, therefore, hardly a viable structural alternative to colonialism, or various forms of totalitarianism.

Bourgeois representative democracy, which talks of political equality among voter-individuals even as it leaves the hierarchical socio-economic relations intact, precludes participatory democracy. Democracy, in such a situation, is chimerical and formal because the anti-dialogic (political-economic) logic of representation, which is constitutive of socio-economic stratification, means that people occupying lower stations of the hierarchy would always be *re-presented* by people above them. In other words, their destinies would be determined by people and institutions that stand apart and above them. Structures and institutions will always determine and *re-present* human beings, never the other way round. The only freedom people have is the freedom to choose who will represent them in those institutions. Representative democracy offers them no freedom to change the structural anti-dialogic logic of *re-presentation* that is manifest through and in the institutions of liberal democracy. There can clearly be no true political equality (of liberties) among individuals without an equality of socio-economic entitlements, and vice-versa. The current system, where *egalité* and *liberté* are notionally on a par but where the latter actually has primacy over the former, has to give way to another order. One that is constituted by a collapse of the two attributes into a singularity that Balibar calls *egaliberté*.

Such obfuscation of the social logic of colonialism and, more importantly, national liberation in post-colonial representative democracies should make us even more attentive to the subtleties of Elias's stance on the issue — a national-liberation movement is no more and no less than a moment of social revolution and class struggle. To that extent, the 'nationalist' struggle of East Bengal against its Pakistani colonizers is for him part of a constellation of various such moments in Bengal's temporal history. Those moments may precede or follow each other in lived time, they may also differ from one another in the idioms in which they express themselves or the authorities they confront. But all of them articulate, either unconsciously or self-consciously, a singular, synchronic tendency: transformation of relations of oppression, exploitation and domination to accomplish autonomy and free association. The manner in which Haddi Khijir views an anti-Pakistan procession he also participates in is revealing.

People have started pouring out from the alleys. From the shanty behind the Nabadwip-Basak Lane, a group of 10-15 men in rags and faded jackets come out. Workers from Shamsuddin's bread factory on Panchbhaighat Lane have left behind the comforting warmth of the tandoor to hit the streets. A group of rickshawpullers has emerged from the Hrishikesh Das Road garage.... The procession of human beings keeps growing in the yellowish-black glow of streetlights and a shiver runs down Khijir's spine. He's certain the old residents of the locality have joined them. But he's unafraid. Call them djinns or specters, today everybody has become one with men.... Residents of Ishwar Das Lane come, accompanied by the students of Bani Bhavan College. Lots of boys from the shoemakers' ghetto next to the municipality office are also here.....Khijir's procession is now opposite Victoria Park. The trees in the park nod their heads affirmatively in response to the slogans. Some sepoys of yore descend from the tall palm trees after freeing themselves from the noose. They too will turn right with the procession. (My translation.).

In Khijir's eyes, the procession, a 'real-life' occurrence in the novel, acquires a dream-like texture with various small collectivities from different spatial and occupational locations of 1969 East Pakistan merging into it. As if this weaving together of spatial and occupational differences into a single fabric of the procession were not enough to establish his conception of 'synchronic' history, Elias ties into it a phenomenon which is separated from the immediate anti-Pakistani upsurge by more than a century. The ghosts of sepoys hanged by the British for their participation in the "mutiny" of 1857 descend from the palm trees of Dhaka to join in. The trope of the procession tells us that Elias does not envisage the continuity of all these struggles as various successive stages of a single ascending history with an idyllic telos. The procession is actually a constellation of struggles bound together by the logic of a single social revolution, albeit manifest through different idioms and political forms in different historical times. This logic of class struggle, it must be pointed out, is not foundational in any phenomenological sense but is only so in the sense of a relational logic intrinsic to capitalism.

The social revolutionary essence of national liberation is Elias's constant preoccupation and it figures in *Khowabnama* as well. In this novel he constructs an account of the Partition (in the east), which does not quite square up with the mainstream historical accounts — whether Bangladeshi, Pakistani or Indian — of the event. He shows that even Muslim League's communal nationalism, which was reactionary to begin with, thrived only by drawing sustenance from the radical politics of the Tebhaga movement. The advances made by League's communal nationalist politics of Pakistan is, as Elias's *Khowabnama* shows, in large measure due to the adoption of Tebhaga's rhetoric by the League. It is no surprise that such rhetoric, given that Tebhaga was a communist-led movement of sharecroppers for firm tenurial security and transformation of the oppressive and exploitative land relations of rural Bengal, had an overt social revolutionary tenor. That was, however, not the only thing the Muslim League of the late 1940s borrowed from Tebhaga. After the retreat of the communists from the movement, the League also got to capitalize on the social disaffection and political anger among the largely poor Muslim peasantry of the region. It, not surprisingly, gave that anger a communal-nationalist turn. We should not forget that the predominantly Muslim landless labourers and sharecroppers in East Bengal gave the movement for Pakistan in that area its crucial mass and strength.

Thus for Elias, national liberation is a dialectic of two moments — a moment of politically expressing social disaffection and class discontent on one hand; and a moment of institutionalisation of nation, reification of national identity and the concomitant repression of the moment of social struggle on the other.

Such a dialectical understanding of national liberation *a la* Elias leaves us with no option but to critically engage with it and other similar identity struggles — neither embrace them fully nor reject them lock, stock and barrel. This engagement should be such that we are able to discern how the idiom (or form) of an identity movement mediates its essence. In other words, when and how does such a movement best express the singular social revolutionary logic embedded in it, and when and how exactly does a movement's identitarian idiom brush it against its essential grain of social revolution by repressing it and distorting its singular expression. For Elias, the idiom of national liberation is important enough not to be rejected. But it is, at the same time, not so significant as to be fully embraced. National liberation is an identitarian moment in the process of social revolution or class struggle. It must, therefore, be recognized as such and then also be dissolved into the process so that the struggle can find its new moment of most accurate expression. In the absence of such awareness, revolutionary politics either risks mistaking such moments for their essential, singular logic (if and when identity politics is fully embraced), or the essential social revolutionary logic itself becomes a particular moment and thereby loses its singular universality (if and when identity politics is completely rejected). In either case, we are left with the triumph of identity, and its logic of congealment through alienation, over the non-identitarian and non-alienated logic of pure becoming. While social revolutionaries will have to pose the logic of pure becoming against the alienating logic of identity formation, this revolutionary operation must be self-reflexively conscious of the fact that identities are as much the various points of appearance of the singular social revolutionary process in its movement through various spatio-temporalities as they are its equally numerous prisons.

The national-liberationist form of the 1969-71 movement in East Pakistan is, in *Sepai*, important to the extent that it's only through this form the basic social revolutionary content of the movement is expressed. The national-liberationist idiom is, however, equally important when it represses and confines its social revolutionary content because that content can be accessed and foregrounded only when we recognize its repressed (absent or unconscious) presence in the conscious form. Such a constellational/'synchronic' conception, which is strictly theoretical and logical, should not be a pretext to paper over the empirical and formal historicity of various struggles, though. We cannot afford to conflate movements that are unconsciously social revolutionary with those that are self-consciously so. A constellational/'structural' view of history is merely meant to foreground the sedimented class reality of non-class, identitarian movements so that the fundamental impulse or aspiration of politics and movements can be underscored, if only to grasp their subsumption, distortion or betrayal. That is vital if the impulse is to be yet again foregrounded on the terrain of critical politics by setting the social revolutionary process free from its various *momentary* prisons. The essence must appear, not disguised as something else, but as its fully conscious self sans all mediatory distortions. It must, however, be borne in mind that the unconscious essence of politics can constitute itself only in relation to the conscious appearance of metapolitics. Its in-itself existence is notional, not real. For, the real is always defined and formed vis-à-vis the symbolic. The point then is that such appearance of the real as real can only be a provisional moment that indicates the actual non-alienated, dialectical and dialogic logic of relationship between the two. Its critical revolutionary function, therefore, is to disabuse us of our understanding, till that moment, that the logic of this relationship is one of separateness, competition and domination.

It is this constellational formation of political resistance that compels Elias in *Sepai* to keep pulling the phenomenon of the Bangladeshi national-liberation struggle towards himself and pushing it away, obsessively doing both at one and the same instant. Such neurotic restlessness is not unusual. For what is constellational history if not an impossible representation of constant dialectical movement — of the singularity of a universal logic splitting into a plurality of particular forms, which once again dissolve into the singularity of the universal, which once again splits, *ad infinitum*. This is multiplicity, which presents differences (particular forms) as same (the singular logic embedded in them) even as it sees and shows the same (the singular logic) manifest by those differences. In such an order of things, the sameness of differences and the differences of the same appear all together and simultaneously.

Ghatak, in sharp contrast to Elias in *Sepai,* is not an obsessive 'multiplicist'. He is, much as he would want to be otherwise, a 'rejectionist' and 'chooser'. His politics and art, in the way they embody his concerns, seem to presume a world of heterogeneous forms that are all complete in themselves. Here *pre*-national 'organic' community is envisaged as a self-contained thing-in-itself, *prior* to and existentially independent of the nation-state. It's, therefore, seen to be completely *separate* from and *outside* the realm of alienating civil society of different individuals. Such a socio-political imagination compels Ghatak to view the preponderance of the nation-state as merely the result of competitive domination of the 'non-alienated' pre-capitalist communitarian *form* by the alienation-fostering bourgeois national *form. Jukti* — which we analyse here because it is characteristically representative of Ghatak's political and aesthetic personality imbued as it was with the trauma of Partition — is an accurate expression of that imaginary. The film shows Neelkantha articulating his criticism of the Bangladeshi national-liberation war; not by engaging with it but by rejecting it for the lost idyll of an organic pre-national community.

For Ghatak, obtaining to an organic, non-alienated state of being is a matter of choosing one form of social organization (pre-capitalist communitarianism) by rejecting another (the liberal nation of citizens), not of critical engagement with bourgeois nationhood, and its logic of alienation, to access the inverse logic of non-alienation immanent in them. So, while Elias sees in the national liberation project possibilities of a social revolution and their simultaneous cooption, for Ghatak all such possibilities exist outside and independent of this struggle which for him is devoid of all revolutionary impulse. That is quite evident in Neelkantha's complete refusal to engage with the movement. He rejects the petty-bourgeois euphoria evoked by the liberation war in West Bengal. He presciently believes that the attendant nationalist fervour would, in the name of erasing religious differences to unite a divided Bengal, do no more than enable the petty-bourgeois elite from both sides to further close ranks against the subalterns.

Yet that belief is born, not through a process of critical engagement with the concrete conjunctural reality of national liberation, but from nostalgia for a non-alienated communitarian idyll that supposedly existed as a tangible material form prior to the advent of nationhood. Neelkantha does not even wish to account for how exactly the Bangladeshi national liberation struggle represses and betrays its social revolutionary impulse. For him a mere declaration of the problem would do. He is shown ranting against the "bourgeoisie" of two Bengals (Indian west and Pakistani/Bangladeshi east) for having lunged the "dagger" of national-liberationist betrayal into the back of the toiling masses. This illustrates quite well how Marxism can become an alibi for romantic communitarianism. And all of Ghatak's films, but particularly *Subarnarekha*, *Komal Gandhar* (*C-Minor*) and *Badi Theke Paliye* (*Escaping Home*), are replete with such examples.

The right statement made, the quest for possibilities of a non-alienated society unfolds — irrespective of the ongoing national liberation war — through a picaresque journey across the rural hinterland of Indian West Bengal. Neelkantha and his itinerant group of three encounter the possibilities of an organic Bengali community in folk art forms (Chau dance and its masks), tribal ways of life, demotic customs, and, last but not least, the unifying principle of the Mother cult and Naxal insurgency. All those experiences are significant in that they confront the modern and genteel linguistic-cultural Bengali 'nationhood' as its gothic, ugly, inchoate and self-destructive instincts, which it has purged itself of. The confrontation is staged to shock the 'nationalist' Bengali out of his culturally smug and complacent being and renew his ontological perception so that they are encountered, not as marginalized externalities of its social present, but as reminders of what Bengaliness was before its destructive and alienating national fate. The confrontation is, by that same turn of logic, equally an intimation of what Bengaliness can be once such a fate is shunned. Ghatak's approach, in his quest for a non-alienated world, is both a priori and transcendental. Pre-capitalist communitarianism is, for him, evidently both a prelapsarian world of organicity lost through the 'original sin' of nationalism, and the redemptive telòs, which can be reached by subordinating the 'sinful' world of nationalism and nation-state to its divine dominion.

Yet, Ghatak's Neelkantha is unable to successfully reclaim that pre-national communitarian organicity, where Bengali 'genteelness' was integrated with and inflected by what it has expelled as common and vulgar in its 'period' of modern nationhood. He finds those common folks — his keepers of a happy and non-alienated communitarian conscience — driven by the alienating logic of competition and hierarchy in their struggle to preserve, ironically enough, their 'organic' identities. They are, therefore, condemned to conduct their struggle in terms of triumph or defeat for their identity. The stubborn refusal of a drunk Santhal, Neelkantha's violent fury notwithstanding, to admit that the local liquor they had been drinking was as much Bengali in provenance as Santhali bears that out.

Ghatak seems oblivious of the fact that the obverse of heterogeneity is homogenisation. While the former is the manifest reality, the latter is its impulse. In a world of heterogeneous forms, constituted by the logic of alienation and competition, the tendency of each of those forms is to always outcompete and dominate the rest in order to establish its homogenizing hegemony. And that would be true in all cases, irrespective of whether one form dominates or the other.

The political struggle that Ghatak appears to conceive is merely about inverting the order of domination — pre-capitalist communitarianism over nationhood — not the erasure of the logic of competitive domination itself. The victory that such a struggle would yield is bound to be pyrrhic and a contradiction in terms. For, the moment the form of 'non-alienated' pre-capitalist community seeks to outcompete and dominate the form of bourgeois nationhood, it accepts its articulation by the logic of capitalist alienation. A pre-capitalist community does not defeat and displace nationhood; it becomes a nation itself.

Clearly, bourgeois nationhood and society have rendered the existence of organic and non-alienated communities *logically* impossible. And the only way to get around this impossibility is to self-consciously deploy the 'memories' of non-alienated pre-capitalism as a provisional ground, within the modern bourgeois social formation, for launching a critique of that logic of alienation. Pier Paolo Pasolini has deployed such politico-aesthetic tactics quite effectively in the films that comprise his *Trilogy of Life*. The cinematic adaptations of *The Decameron* (1971), *Canterbury Tales* (1972) and *Arabian Nights* (1974) — all carefully chosen mediaeval tracts of fables and parables on love and eroticism — are meant to be not so much depictions of communitarian manners of real love as an allusion through those depictions to the impossibility of love in an alienated and alienating capitalist society. Given that Italy of the early '70s was still largely in the cusp of transition from rural pre-modernity to modern urban-centric capitalism, the relevance of such tactics need not be overstated.

But that was not Ghatak's way. His politics, dogged by the self-contradictions of its aprioristic/transcendental and parahistorical premises, left him with no choice but to fail, romanticize 'revolutionary' failure and unabashedly depict it. Such failure to reach the telos of an organic community arises from the impossibility of posing non-alienation as an end-in-itself. To envisage an end would be to signal the triumph of one moment over the rest. It would, by the same token, be an eternalised congealment of pure, unalienated and infinite becoming in that one moment. That would spell both alienation and competitive domination. Impossibility and failure on that score must, therefore, be read as alluding to the logical-critical functionality of 'pre-capitalist' communitarianism, vis-à-vis the logic of capitalist alienation. That, however, would be our "catastrophic" (Adorno; 2005, pp 42) reading of Jukti. The film itself, thanks to its reification of failure, precludes such critical self-reflexivity. It's this self-consciousness that distinguishes Elias's politics and art from Ghatak's. The difference is most telling in the way they approach and deploy myths in their artistic creations. But to comprehend this difference, and particularly Elias's approach to myth, it is necessary that we unravel its politico-theoretical armature.

HISTORICISING MYTH : A THEORETICAL DETOUR

To appreciate the place of myths in Elias's politico-aesthetic paradigm, we need to understand the idea of myth as a kind of 'synchronic' or 'structural' history, which "has nothing to do with a present, eternal or otherwise, and is not to be grasped in terms of lived or existential time". (Jameson; 2007, pp 89.) This understanding would, among other things, also help us distinguish Elias's approach to myth and its 'pre-modern' order from that of Ghatak's. It would also serve to ground their respective political positions on nation, national-liberation and communitarianism — especially with regard to Partition of Bengal and the Bangladeshi national-liberation struggle — in the realm of theory.

In Elias, myth is imagined as a reality, which is absent in lived or existential time. The historiography, constitutive of such a vision, no longer envisages History as the unfolding of a narrative of occurrences in a temporal continuum. Instead, it renders History into a structure where everything is present all together: as much the manifest empirical reality of existence, as what this reality absents or represses and which therefore lies immanent in it. History becomes a kaleidoscope with all patterns inherent in it, even as the visibility (or not) of each of those patterns is contingent on how the kaleidoscope turns. It is like the (Japanese) fan of Benjamin's (1986, pp 6) memory, which keeps opening endlessly because no image can be entirely satisfactory as each image can be unfolded. For instance, here the historical image of existential reality can unfold into the image of what this reality has repressed, which in turn can once again unfold into its negative reality ad infinitum. Conversely, the fan in its folded moment holds all those infinite possibilities and is, therefore, simultaneously an expression of the image that is visible in its folded state and those that it can unfold into. In such circumstances, a myth can become its own critical-negative ground and, by extension, also that of the system that has constructed it as a myth. Myth can clearly cease to be myth. That should not, however, be confused with the affirmation of a myth's literal meaning.

To simply claim that a myth is true would be to accept the determinate mode — constitutive of existential time — that has designated it thus. Never mind that such designation is meant to denigrate its ontology as an impossible fable, and deny its epistemology as false. Such belief in the literalness of a myth would, then, be as much of a non-critical acceptance of existential time as when the truth and/or possibility of that myth is emphatically rejected. Clearly, all knowledge and experience in lived time, whether they exist in the form of dematerialised ideas or are instituted as sensory-empirical materiality, are theoretical objects of the prevailing determinate mode within which they have been produced. Clearly then, critical-theoretical reality of a myth should not only be distinguished from its literal reality, it should be seen as inverting the latter's order in its entirety.

More accurately, reconstitution of myth as knowledge of its own theoretical-critical negativity should be seen as the production of a new theoretical object within a determinate mode that is different and discrete from the determinate mode that designates it as myth and is constitutive of our lived time.

To talk either of myths or the critical-theoretical knowledge immanent in them without first seeing them as specific theoretical objects constituted within their respective determinate modes would, if we were to follow in Balibar's (1999, pp 203) footsteps, be akin to Marx writing the first line of *The Communist Manifesto* — "The history of all hitherto existing society is the history of class struggle." It would, to paraphrase the French Marxist for our purposes, not be the first statement of our theory of the critical knowledge of myths, it would only "summarize the raw material of (our) work of transformation" of myths. The inspiration for this work of transformation can be drawn from Althusser and Balibar's (1997, pp 225) Marx for whom "the definition of every mode of production" is "a *combination* of (always the same) elements which are only notional elements unless they are put into relation with each other according to a determinate mode...". This also affords the possibility of "periodizing the modes of production according to a principle of *variation* of these combinations...".

And what are these different determinate modes if not various language-systems with their own singular rules of syntax and metaphor. Those different rules become manifest when apparently the same syntax, turn of phrase and/or vocabulary come to connote different orders of relationships among the same (notionally) constitutive elements in different discursive or determinate modes. And such discursive differences in connotation for what appears to be the same form of language must be ascribed to unique and singular sets of social practices that underpin and animate the language-form within their respective constitutive determinate modes. In short, each one of those language-systems (determinate modes) envisages a pattern of connections among elements unique and specific to it.

A myth should, then, be defined as a certain specific combination of notional elements, brought together in a certain relationship by the determinate mode of existential time. And its transformation into what can be defined as critical-theoretical knowledge can be understood, according to the principle of variation, as a change in connections and relations among the same elements within a different determinate mode. Balibar's (1997, pp 226) contention that Marx's analysis of a 'combination' (mode of production) was the analysis of "a system of 'synchronic' connexions obtained by variation" implies "the possibility of an *a priori* science of the modes of production, a science of *possible* modes of production, whose realization in real-concrete history would depend on the result of a throw of the dice or the action of an optimum principle". Considering that we are concerned here with understanding both myth and the critical real function it plays in Elias's novels, should we not extend the horizons of Balibar's "a priori science" to also include actual and possible modes of reality, knowledge and experience?

If myth is no more than a theoretical object produced within and by the determinate mode of bourgeois science, rationality and, most importantly, modern secular-democracy, it follows that outside such a mode its status as myth would be completely notional. It also follows, therefore, that within another determinate mode the connections among notional elements — which had in the preceding mode been constituted as myth — would get reorganized differently (according to the principle of variation) to produce a specific theoretical object which is assigned a different ontological-epistemological status of, say, non-myth. Once this theoretical possibility is established, the constitution, or signification, of the critical-negative ontology of myth as it were can be grasped better. The question now is, what would the motive force of this shift — from one determinate mode (of bourgeois rationality and secularism) to another (that of its critique) — be. Or, what impels the envisioning of this critical determinate mode? Unless that question is raised and an attempt is made to meaningfully answer it, we would remain blind, allegedly like Althusser and Althusserians, to the booby-trap of 'theoreticism'. Balibar's "throw of the dice or the action of an optimum principle" clearly needs to be grounded more rigorously.

Integral to such a line of inquiry is the question of agency. For, something has to impel someone. Put more simply, there has to be an agent, who is propelled by some force, to 'found' a determinate mode, in this case the critical determinate mode. Let us understand this interaction between the agent and his motive force more clearly. The agent in the process of embodying and practising the consciousness of myth, and all other forms of knowledge constituted by the established determinate mode, could come to a point where he realizes that some or all forms of knowledge constituted by that mode militate against his 'true' self. This 'trueness' of self — which simultaneously and naturally 'falsifies' existential time, its realities and their determinate mode — is nothing but a function of resistance against the domination and determination of lived time. Clearly then, truths and falsehoods are no more and no less than representations of domination and struggle. Better still, they are conceptualisations of political practice of oppression and/

or resistance. In a fundamental sense therefore, all questions are questions of politics and power struggle, albeit disguised in the 'true-false' and/or 'right-wrong' idioms of ethics and knowledge respectively. Foucault — whose theory of discursive regimes of discourse has a strong methodological affinity with Althusser's philosophy of determinate modes — sought to indicate precisely this masking or articulation of power by knowledge and ethics when he self-reflexively proclaimed, "I have never written anything but fictions." This statement, contrary to what our postmodern friends might want to claim, is not a clarion call to political and ethical relativism. Why else would Foucault's intellectual peer, Deluze (2007, pp 98), have responded thus: "But never has fiction produced such truth and reality."

Foucault's theory clearly needs to be grasped in all its complexity. His contention that "a statement has a 'discursive object' which does not derive in any sense from a particular state of things, but stems from the statement itself" (Deluze; 2007, pp 8) does not imply that different knowledge-systems and experiences in lived time can have equal validity. Instead, he seems to suggest, through an implied dialectical logic, that an object of discourse, precisely because it has no reality outside the discursive field of that discourse, must have the freedom (power) to be reconstituted/resignified within a new discursive field as a completely different object with different meanings, uses and a new ontological reality.

Foucault's theory of discursive fields — if seen as a critical intervention in the domain of knowledge and its production at a concrete socio-historical moment — is a problematising rap on the knuckles of the modern Hegelian hierarchy of disciplines. In such a disciplinary scheme, a knowledge-system or discipline constitutes and defines itself only through a differential turn vis-à-vis all other disciplines, both lower and higher than it on the knowledge ladder. It's hardly surprising that such a situation should have institutionalised the violation of autonomous discursiveness of knowledge fields. This means that discourses do not appear as their own essence. Equally, objects of one discursive field have no power to move into another field, of which they can become the founding event even as they are reconstituted within it as new theoretical objects. In Foucauldian terms, the tendency of knowledge to become its own surface so that it can reside nowhere else but on it is curbed. Modern surfaces have, by becoming repressive lids, created their own depths which they then deign to express and distort.

Foucault's formulation is then a critique of an order of discourse integral to the capitalist political economy of exchange values, which engenders competition, alienation, hierarchy and dominance, and thus quells the constant becoming of an autonomous subject. His theory of discursive discourses must, in that context, be read as an ethics for a yet-to-emerge moment of socialized knowledge production, where the political economy of use value would come into its own. It would be a world, not of static and differential heterogeneities, but of dynamic and organic multiplicity.

This attempt to discover, or shall we say invent, a 'Marxian' Foucault was doubtless a digression. But it is a productive one in that it enables us to foreground the essential relationship between knowledge/ethics and political power. In so doing we get the key to open the agency-motive force deadlock, vis-à-vis the emergence of a new determinate mode of critical knowledge. The political domination that individual/s from certain strata (or class) in an empirically existing social formation are likely to experience while embodying the knowledge-objects of its determinate mode can push them to resist such domination, and eventually the selfhood and knowledge that such domination imposes on them to strengthen its sway. Such resistance confers on them an evanescently autonomous subjectivity that impels them to imagine a new determinate mode of critical knowledge and being. This mode of reflection and practice rearranges the connections between the elements to simultaneously produce new theoretical objects, and a knowledge that can be said to be in concert with, indeed emerges organically from, their 'true' being. Even as it does that, the new mode breaks with the established determinate mode of existential time, which through and because of that break is critically designated as 'false'. But this account, its explanatory usefulness notwithstanding, is both mechanical and dialectically provisional. Worse, it does not pass muster with the Althusserian framework of structural causality. Such an explanation, whereby the emergence of a new determinate mode is made contingent on an autonomous agency completely precluded by the idea of determinate modes, becomes the *deus ex machina* of the Althusserian tangle. And it is condemned to play that role as long as Althusser's framework is not clarified in its conjunctural context.

Let us begin with Balibar's (1997, pp 252) tellingly limiting declaration on that score: "For each practice and for each transformation of that practice, they are the different forms of individuality which can be defined on the basis of its combination structure." His statement clearly precludes the possibility that a subject's revolutionary critical practice would induce it to imagine a new determinate mode of critical knowledge. For, the philosopher has subordinated subjectivity to the "combination structure" (or determinate mode) it was meant to found. Yet the problem remains: Althusser and Balibar's theory of combination structure does not ostensibly explain why or how a determinate mode of critical knowledge comes into being by breaking with the determinate mode of lived bourgeois knowledge. To say that revolutionary practice gives rise to the critical determinate mode that makes revolutionary practice possible amounts to no more than an absurdly un-self-conscious expression of the problem of infinite regress. That would, however, be an inevitable pitfall so long as problems of knowledge are posed only in conceptual terms. For, human language, in which all concepts are necessarily formulated, conceals metaphysics of linear temporality and causality. The problem can be overcome only if we see the two apparently irreconcilable and thus undialectical formulations of the relationship between structure (or theory) and agency (or practice) — where either structure can give rise to practice or practice can found structure — as conceptually frozen halves of a dynamic dialectical whole. That whole is more than the sum of its two halves as in motion each half is both itself and the other at the same time. Ilyenkov's (2008, pp 37) understanding of the abstract and the concrete, and the dialectic between them, could in this instance be illuminating.

"The concrete in thinking also appears, according to Marx's definition, in the form of combination (synthesis) of numerous definitions. A logically coherent system of definitions is precisely that 'natural' form in which concrete truth is realised in thought. Each of the definitions forming part of the system naturally reflects only a part, a fragment, an element, an aspect of the concrete reality — and that is why it is abstract if taken by itself, separately from other definitions. In other words, the concrete is realised in thinking through the abstract through its own opposite, and is impossible without it. But that is, in general, the rule rather than an exception in dialectics. Necessity is in just the same kind of relation with chance essence with appearance, and so on."

To that list we ought to add 'theory with practice' and 'structure with agency'. We need to follow Ilyenkov (and Marx) to realise the concrete by thinking through the abstract of structure (or theory) through its own opposite of agency (or practice). The concrete, dialectical and dynamic whole would, in this case, be praxis, where its two fragments of theory and practice are themselves and each other simultaneously. It could be argued in a similar vein, that Althusser and Balibar's determinate mode of knowledge is both the product and producer of its own practice. And that this practice is as much its theoretical object as it is its singular founding event.

In any case, we should not overlook the fact that Balibar and Althusser's intervention was at an 'anthropomorphic' conjuncture within Marxist politics and theory. To that extent, their revolutionary intent to effectively confront the threat this conjuncture posed to Marxism in terms of evacuating it of all its historical materialist content and class struggle itself cannot surely be faulted. The anthropomorphism of a certain preponderant strain of "humanistic Marxism" had emphasized the problem of alienation of the individual by reifying and eternalising the historical individuality of bourgeois civil society and liberal-democracy. This amounted to wiping off, both deliberately and otherwise, the traces of historical production or constitution of individuality. Althusser and Balibar's response, not incorrectly, was to render the production of the Individual and various other historical individualities visible. And that led them to stress heavily, perhaps excessively, on the virtually de-emphasised objectivist aspect (determinate mode or combination structure) of Marxism. Their tactical attempt to give precedence to structural causality over practice and human subjectivity, if only to respond to the pressing revolutionary needs of their moment, did not blind them to the larger dialectical strategy, though. And that becomes evident when we contrast Althusser and Balibar's 'structuralism' with that of the structuralists.

In the latter, the basic units or elements (mytheme, phoneme, episteme, etc) are positive determinants of various combinatories. They have a meaning a priori to the various systems they constitute. In Althusser's 'structuralism', however, elements outside their determinate mode have merely a notional existence. They become real, or acquire any meaning, only in relation to each other in a determinate mode of knowledge, politics or practice. The privileging of connections between elements and their variations over the elements themselves, shows that Althusser's determinate mode is only a pseudo-structure. Considering that relations, connections and their variations are, unlike the a priori elements of the structuralists, not conceptual fixities, it would be safe to claim that Althusser's structure formed and framed by such mobilities is no more than a conceptual-linguistic schema that mimics the dialectic of historical motion.

A couple of examples, which show how myths and 'true historical' knowledge can both be displaced from the determinate mode of instrumentalised bourgeois rationality into its critical mode where they are reconstituted as different theoretical objects, would be in order. Let's first train our sights on what is known as pre-capitalist communitarianism.

The determinate mode of existential time — which is the time of representative democracy, civil society, nation-states and capitalism — has constituted and signified 'pre-capitalism' as a thoroughly stratified and oppressive theoretical object. That does not, however, mean that this object, which can also be called 'pre-capitalist communitarianism' inhabits existential time only as a dematerialised idea. Its constitution as a stratified and oppressive object is also evident in sensory-empirical terms. The articulation of pre-capitalist communities within and by the determinate mode of capitalism is manifest in how various traditional, 'pre-capitalist' identities such as castes and religious communities have actually been put into relations of mutual hostility and domination by the logic of competition that arises from that determinate mode. In such circumstances, a critical determinate mode, constitutive of a possible time outside the one that we inhabit, can reconstitute pre-capitalism as a non-alienated and organic social formation. That is exactly what many of Pasolini's films, especially the ones cited above, do.

At the risk of doing some violence to our cardinal framework of determinate modes and theoretical objects, let us provisionally adopt the methods of empirical history to better understand the stratification-organicity binary in pre-capitalist communities. That would, if anything, only help us shore up the validity of our framework. Pre-capitalist communities have, in temporal-empirical history, been both stratified and organic. This strange paradox arises from the fact that while in economic terms those societies were stratified as surplus would be extracted by force, in psycho-cultural terms their ordinary denizens felt much less alienated than the average individual-citizen of modern civil society. After all, caste or religious community, which can be extremely coercive and totalitarian at functional level, also does give people even now a sense of familial closeness and social security. The competitive logic of capitalism has, in articulating the remnants of pre-capitalist communities, de-emphasised their psycho-cultural aspects even while accentuating their oppressive and hierarchical socio-economic dimensions.

Now for myth. Ernst Cassirer (1953, pp 4-5), one of the key movers of the Neo-Kantian current in philosophy, employs the methods of comparative philology (or linguistics) to show how the Greek myth of Daphne and Apollo was, for the ancient Greeks, not a fictional myth at all but lived reality.

"Daphne, who is saved from Apollo's embraces by the fact that

her mother, the Earth, transforms her into a laurel tree. ..it is only the history of language that can make this myth "comprehensible," and give it any sort of sense. Who was Daphne? In order to answer this question we must resort to etymology, that is to say we must investigate the history of the word. "Daphne" can be traced back to the Sanskrit Ahana, and Ahana means in Sanskrit the redness of dawn. As soon as we know this, the whole matter becomes clear. The story of Phoebus (Apollo) and Daphne is nothing but a description of what one may observe everyday: first, the appearance of the dawnlight in the eastern sky, then the rising of the sun-god who hastens after his bride, then the gradual fading of the red dawn at the touch of the fiery rays, and finally its death or disappearance in the bosom of Mother Earth. So the decisive condition for the development of the myth was not the natural phenomenon itself, but rather the circumstance that the Greek word for the laurel and the Sanskrit word for the dawn are related; this entails with a sort of logical necessity the identification of the beings they denote."

That an ancient Greek account of an observable natural phenomenon becomes for us, modern human beings, a myth is because the same set of linguistic statements are loaded with two completely different kinds of connotative charge within their respectively distinct discursive-linguistic modes. Cassirer (1953, pp 5) himself suggests as much when he approvingly quotes Max Mueller: "Mythology is inevitable, it is natural, it is an inherent necessity of language, if we recognize in language the outward form and manifestation of thought; it is in fact the dark shadow which language throws upon thought and which can never disappear till language becomes entirely commensurate with thought, which it never will." This implies, dialectically, that reality will always be apprehended through its symbolization in language (discourse and/or practice) even as it will slip through its grasp like sand to necessitate its constant resignification. We can in terms of the discussion here, also take it to be an account of the perpetual shifting of determinate modes, which will constantly vary the pattern of relationship among their elements to resignify and reconstitute them as new objects.

Zizek (2003, pp 6) intends to emphasize precisely that when

he summons Robert Pfaller's authority to argue that "the direct belief in a truth that is subjectively fully assumed ("Here I stand!") is a modern phenomenon, in contrast to traditional beliefs-through-distance, like politeness or rituals. Pre-modern societies did not believe directly, but through distance, and this explains, for instance, why Enlightenment critics misread "primitive" myths — they first took the notion that a tribe originated from a fish or a bird as a literal direct belief, then rejected it as stupid, "fetishist," naïve." But it is not Zizek's to merely prove how myths can be displaced from the determinate mode of bourgeois Enlightenment to be reconstituted as another possible existential reality. He is also implying the political necessity of that shift and displacement, if only to effect a critical resistance against the domination of the determinate mode of instrumentalised rationality and its constitutive bourgeois political economy.

The examples above indicate that there can be times and historical worlds, parallel to and outside the history of existential time, to which we, its inhabitants, can escape even as our ontologies are transfigured in the process. It is, however, equally evident that we can discern such possible realities — which are supposed to be constitutive of critical histories vis-à-vis the historical reality of existential time — only in their representations. We are constrained to access their possible *existence* only through the representational resources of language, discourse and practice available within lived time. Possible realities, as a result, come to inhabit the existential time of which they are presumed to be alternatives of. They thus end up articulating their logic of non-alienation and non-competition, paradoxically enough, through the theories, discourses and practices of alienation and competition constitutive of existential time. In such circumstances, we must learn to look *through* how they are being articulated (by the existential logic of alienation and competition) to *see* what they intend to articulate (the possible logic of non-alienation and non-competition).

All ideologies, including those that seek to critique the alienated/commodified reality (or ideology) of existential time of capitalism, are discernible only as commodities. Their representation within this time of capitalism, constituted by its regime of differential exchange values, renders them thus. This clearly means the relative importance of critical ideologies in capitalist society would be completely contingent on their valorisation through competition. In such circumstances, it would be unlikely that a critical ideology, which embodies the logic of non-alienation, would have many takers. The market would simply not ascribe as much value to an ideological commodity that threatens its survival, as it imputes to one (of alienation and competition) that constitutes and reinforces it.

And yet because the existential significance of such ideologies is contingent on the hope that they will overcome this logic of alienated and hierarchical valorisation, they need to create a demand for themselves. A demand that outstrips the demand for the alienating logic constitutive of lived time. This demand has to be for, not what the critical ideological commodity can immediately offer, but what it promises to deliver. It has to create a demand, not for possession but for hope. Hope, however, cannot in this instance be based on blind faith or superstition. It must produce proof. A critical ideology can deliver that proof by generating, what Alain Badiou (2006, pp x) terms, "reality effect" within existential time and its structure of reality. This effect of its non-alienated, non-competitive historical reality can be produced only if the ideology — irrespective of whether it is a conceptual/aesthetic formulation or a mode of practice — self-reflexively includes within itself the historical location and process of its real emergence. It would thereby allude to the trans-representational, non-alienated logic implicit in it. A logic that effects complete and perfect consonance between essence and appearance, or reality and its representation. Such self-reflexivity, needless to say, would have to be a function of the style and/or technique of practice and/or conceptual formulation. The need for a 'theory of allusion to the implicit', to account for and measure the radical capacity of various seemingly disparate revolutionary practices and/or concepts, can hardly be overstated.

THE RETURN: GHATAK'S FAILURE AND ELIAS'S DEFERRED SUCCESS

It's on this terrain of reality effects and 'allusion to the implicit' that Elias's politico-aesthetic endeavour to reconstitute myths as critical-negative knowledge of our existential history must be comprehended and distinguished from Ghatak's 'mythic' vision of lived reality. Elias's narrative strategy or representational technique in *Khowabnama*, for instance, enables him to extract from certain traditional and syncretic folklore and fables of rural East Bengal the effect of a reality they critically and negatively posit. His use of the *khowab* (dream) trope to depict myths is meant to accomplish exactly that. He shows Tamijer Baap, a key character in the novel, encounter those fables in his dreams, thereby transforming those *fictions* into a reality of their own. After all, the dreamer experiences dreams as if they were real occurrences in a world he can only enter through sleep by leaving the world of wakeful, existential reality behind. There is then a world where dreams can cease being dreams to become reality. For, people know they had been dreaming only when the dream is over and they have woken up. The world of dreams, when a person is encountering it in his sleep, is absolutely real. It's, however, equally true that dream is not a thing-in-itself. Its existence, contingent on sleep, is bound to wakefulness in an inverse relationship. In short, dream and wakefulness are not separate realms-in-themselves, but are inflected by one another.

The reality-myth relationship, posed by Elias as one between wakefulness and dream, is rendered through this dialectic into a relationship between two realities — one existential while the other absent but possible. It also means that existential reality can travel down the strand of its inverse relationship with dream — which is simultaneously rendered into yet another, possible reality — to *become* that. The distinction between 'myth' (as fiction or transcendental faith) and 'reality' (as existential fact) is, as a result, obliterated. Such obliteration is for, example, evident in the way the ghost of a local Muslim ascetic — apparently killed in the anti-British Fakir-Sanyasi rebellions of late 18th-early 19th century — and other associated fabulistic events keep irrupting into and transfiguring the existential reality of Tamijer Baap in his sleepwalking reveries and activities. Those fables are, in the process, transformed from being fantastic, awe- and faith-inspiring tales into stirring memories of glorious resistance against oppression. Needless to say, the extractive oppression of the British East India Company of 18th-19th century and the exploitative ways of the local landlords and rich peasants of the 1940s are, their separation in time notwithstanding, integrated into the same historical-logical constellation. It's, however, through mendicant Cherag Ali, Tamijer Baap's spiritual mentor, that Elias is able to establish this logic of dissolution on firmer foundations. A dream-reader, Cherag Ali interprets dreams through the prism of doggerels and limericks of his mystic tradition as intimations of things to come in the existential-temporal continuum. His reading of dreams grounds them — together with the incantatory magic of his "authorless", mystic rhymes — in lived reality. Once again dreams and fables, thanks to such interpretation, are deemed real possibilities. They lose their mysterious depths, because of this interpretative turn, to become their own *real*, comprehensible surfaces.

What changes, therefore, are not merely the ontologies of myth and existential reality but, more importantly, the relationship between the two. In fact, the two different ontological situations — of myth-reality on one hand, and possible reality-existential reality on the other — are functions of two different orders of relationship. In the first case, it's a relationship of alienation, domination and one-way determination. Existential reality dominates over myth (or dream), as if the latter were a realm separate from and outside it, and determines its meaning by denying it the possibility of expressing any reality other than the one it has been framed in. In the second instance, the relationship is between two different moments of the same process. Here, lived reality and what it has designated as myth are not separate from each other but are like two points in a flowing stream. Different points that flow into each other to become one.

Ghatak's idea that lived reality conceals mythic sub-structures, which determine it, is in sharp contrast to this dialectical-logical approach towards myths. If we were to follow Ghatak's aesthetic-philosophical logic and realize, not merely in ideas but in our existence, the mythic archetype of our lived reality, it would mean that myths become existential reality. But do we then stop there as if the hidden truth of our existence has become apparent and our 'true' selves have, in the process, been rendered free? The answer, as far as Ghatak is concerned, is a resounding yes. In *Meghe Dhaka Tara* (Cloud-capped Star), the crushed and exploited existence of protagonist Nita, a typical representative of Bengali womanhood, is sought to be shown and explained fully in terms of the figure of Mother goddess, a mythic image of the self-sacrificing provider in Bengali culture and imagination. Someone could, of course, claim through a dialectical reading of the film that Ghatak has historicized the myth of the Mother Goddess in terms of the exploitative reality of the post-Partition refugee Bengali woman. And that would, without doubt, be an honourable revolutionary intention to ascribe to the text of the film. It's, however, equally our task to know whether, and how far, does this intention of the text coincide with the intention of the author.

The absolute pessimism in which the filmmaker steeps the possibility of Nita's emancipation, by evoking a melodramatic ambience of despair towards the end of the film, clearly suggests that there is no escape for her from her myth-ordained fate. It, therefore, also shows that for Ghatak, the historicisation of lived reality is merely its reduction to a mythic archetype. The filmmaker's aesthetic imaginary anticipates, arguably, his impossible, failure-ridden political project of establishing the domination of 'organic' communitarianism over alienating nationhood, paradoxically to end the domination and exploitation of modern bourgeois nations. Even revolution becomes, in *Nagarik* (Citizen), a matter of fate. The film, true to Ghatak's philosophical-aesthetic programme of unearthing mythic sub-structures of lived reality, appears to suggest that the exploitation, progressive immiserisation of the refugees from East Bengal, and the consequent socio-political unrest on the streets of Calcutta, is no more than the playing out of the mythic *yuga*-ic cycle.

Ghatak's (2000, pp 36) mythic a priorism is starkly evident in this theorization of his cinematic aesthetics:

"Since Depth Psychology and Comparative Mythology have laid bare certain fundamental workings of the human psyche as ever recurring constellations of primordial archetypes, our task today has become easier.

"We now know, all that creates art in the human psyche also creates religion; a medicine man, a 'shaman', a 'rishi' a 'poet', and a 'village woman possessed by seizure' are, fundamentally, set in motion by the same or similar kinds of unconscious forces.

"And these forces are the very ones which are continually nourishing the subjective psychic bond, giving an inner subjective correspondence to the objective creation around us.

"It follows that all art is subjective. Any work of art is the artist's subjective approximation of the reality around him. It is a sort of reaction set in motion by the creative impulse of the human unconscious."

This theorization is complete if it's seen merely as an attempt by an artist to explain his art as an expression of his moment. But read as a politico-aesthetic programme it is, at best, partial and at worst, undialectically mysterian. None can dispute the fact that "any work of art is the artist's subjective approximation of the reality around him". Yet, that statement can sum up a revolutionary philosophical aesthetic programme in its completeness only if it manages to yet again collapse that subjectivity into its constitutive objective reality and, most importantly, its political praxis. In Ghatak's (2000, pp 37) imagination, "dialectics is *born*: the interplay of the subjective and the objective" "in the objectivization of this essentially subjective element". (Emphasis mine.)

This understanding of dialectics as merely the primacy of subjective over objective robs it of its processual logic by rendering it into a phenomenon and an ontology: an eternalized closure of the process of infinite becoming in one of its moments. That amounts to the un-self-conscious triumph of phenomenology and its logic of alienation over the idea of subtracted ontology and its logic of pure becoming. Ghatak's art, and his aesthetic programme, do not radiate self-awareness. They do not seem to express the idea that mythic sub-structures of lived historical time are useful only to the extent that they indicate, through their negative-critical and possible reality, the transformation of the logic of alienation, opposition and oppression into an unalienated logic of horizontal process.

Myth, as Elias has shown, can seek to free itself of its falsified ontology, imposed on it by the repressive workings of existential reality, not by being existential reality, but by allusively critiquing the logic of alienation that is constitutive of beings and the idea of ontology. The critical power of myths, vis-à-vis existential reality, lies not so much in their having become empirical reality of existence from the absent negative reality they were, but in the logic of processual becoming that this transformation alludes to.

This lack of self-awareness and self-reflexivity in Ghatak's cinema and his politics could be located in his theoretical dependence on psychologist Carl Jung's idea of the collective unconscious. For Jung, unlike Freud, the unconscious is not existentially constituted by the conscious mind and in inverse relation to it; it is a kind of a collection of man's animal instincts that exists as a thing-in-itself and prior to the advent of the consciousness of rational human being. The unconscious in Jung is a misnomer. To call it pre-conscious would actually make it more theoretically consistent.

But it's not as if the awareness of a non-alienated relational logic between myth and existential reality as two moments of the same process of constant becoming is discernible in Elias's novel (*Khowabnama*) as the self-consciousness of characters who embody it. The sleepwalking reveries of Tamijer Baap, or the Delphic reading of dreams by Cherag Ali are, without doubt, moments when myths irrupt into lived history obliterating themselves and that history in the process. But those moments, considering that they happen to them as individuals, do no more than allude to the possibility of such obliteration for their entire community. The two personas in question are characterologically constrained to merely experience that possibility as individuals, not access and foreground the revolutionary transformative impulse that resides in the sediments of their ecstasy and intoxication. Those characters and their 'obliterative' aptitudes are, as a result, condemned to be included on the margins of oppressive existential time as suspect, despicable, frightening, irrational and even false. Such differential inclusion also involves repression of the possible realities their aptitudes and personas posit and, as a consequence, pre-empts all efforts towards the collective realisation of those possibilities. Those characters, notwithstanding the critical-obliterative potential inherent in their mystic-hallucinatory energies of intoxication, are condemned to be oppressed and dominated by the lived time of rich peasants such as Sharafat Mandal and the power-hungry and effete politicians of the Muslim League and the undivided Communist Party of India respectively. This is in large measure due to their historical lack of awareness about the revolutionary potential of their aptitude for 'intoxication', which by itself is never good enough. For, as Benjamin (1986, pp 190) says, "..to place the accent exclusively on it would be to subordinate the methodical and disciplinary preparation for revolution entirely to a praxis oscillating between fitness exercises and celebration in advance. Added to this is an inadequate, undialectical conception of the nature of intoxication... Any serious exploration of occult, surrealistic, phantasmagoric gifts and phenomena presupposes a dialectical intertwinement to which a romantic turn of mind is impervious. For histrionic or fanatical stress on the mysterious side of the mysterious takes us no further; we penetrate the mystery only to the degree that we recognize it in the everyday world, by virtue of a dialectical optic that perceives the everyday as impenetrable, the impenetrable as everyday."

The knowledge of a non-alienated, dialectical relationship between myth and existential reality is, therefore, expressed in the novel through the narrativising voice of its author. This authorial voice does not, however, come across as an expression a priori to and independent of the happenings in the novel. It is, instead, their constitutive narrative glue. Elias's representational strategy, which depicts myth as dream to indicate the non-alienated relationship between existential reality and myth, emanates from his politics of engaging with existential time without either fully embracing or rejecting it. To that extent, his determinate/discursive mode, within which the discourse of myth is reordered, and articulated as a critique of the alienating logic of existential time, is constituted by the author's affirmative identification with the militant praxis of classical revolutionary politics. And to this Elias alludes, self-reflexively, through the character of Keramat Ali, a poor peasant who attempts to takes mystic Cherag Ali's poetic tradition forward. Keramat, purportedly inspired by Cherag Ali, becomes a wandering minstrel in a Tebhaga-struck swathe of East Bengal. There is, however, one very crucial difference between the "student" and his "master". The former does not, like the latter, recite poetry bestowed on him by a depersonalised mystic and mythic tradition. He is a singer of new, self-composed songs whose authorship he unabashedly claims. His songs are obviously not interpretations of dreams and myths. They are an expression of his community's new existential reality: the uprising of poor sharecroppers and landless labourers against an exploitative and oppressive landed gentry, and subsequently the Muslim League's demand for an "egalitarian" Pakistan. Keramat's continuity and break with Cherag Ali, at one and the same time, portrays the transformation of the mystic-mendicant historical individuality of Cherag Ali into a different historical individuality, that of a revolutionary poet. The latter is both a doer (militant) and a thinker (poet), and is thus part and parcel of a praxis, which engenders the reality and logic of pure, unalienated becoming against the dominant existential reality of alienation and exploitation. This praxis, and the militant/poetic historical individuality constitutive of its revolutionary mode, is born out of a community's urge to emancipate itself from oppression and render its repressed ontology and epistemology valid. It's, simultaneously, the event that triggers the awareness of such oppression and alienation. Here we have a tangible example of something we dealt with in the abstract above: the dialectic of how a new determinate mode is founded by an evental/revolutionary subject, which is simultaneously constituted as an individuality of this revolutionary mode of doing and reflection. But what is perhaps most important is that the two characters of Cherag Ali and Keramat Ali, united by a troubadour's tradition but separated by the break that Keramat has introduced into it, constitute a narrative device that Elias employs to show how an oppressed and exploited individual, when he becomes a militant against such depredations, breaks with existential history to inhabit a different historical reality and time. The determinate mode constitutive of this new reality and time puts him (an element) in a new relationship with all others (remaining elements) of his society and, in the process, assigns him with a new ontological self. Militant-poet Keramat Ali is, therefore, none other than Late Cherag Ali, who has broken with his earlier mystic-mendicant self to become a revolutionary bard. And this break happens because Cherag Ali's dream-reading vocation had made him into an inflection point between existential reality and its critical-negative knowledge in myths. Thus mystic poet Cherag Ali has, in the process of becoming militant poet Keramat, merely turned his face away from the oppressive reality of existential wakefulness to travel down the strand of inverse relationship that links this wakefulness to mythic mystic dreams, if only to realize in empirical-material terms the critique of the alienating logic of existential time that those myths had negatively posed in his 'mystic' interpretations.

The Althusserian homology of the break between Early Cherag Ali and Late Cherag Ali a la Keramat, can be extended to show that Elias — whose *Khowabnama* posits a new determinate mode within which myths are reconstituted as critical-negative knowledge of the existential reality of 1940s' Bengal — is none other than Late Keramat Ali. He could perhaps, by that same logic, also be called Very Late Cherag Ali. *Khowabnama*'s critical determinate mode is not possible without the revolutionary praxis of Tebhaga, whose legacy Elias inherited. It's only in and through its evental praxis — which presented a lived, material, empirical critique and alternative to the alienating and exploitative logic of 1940s' Bengal — that mythic 'fictions' could be re-imagined as realities repressed by an oppressive and alienating existential reality. They could, therefore, also be posed as the negative-critical knowledge of such reality. There is, however, a small problem. A struggle like Tebhaga is bound to be articulated by the existential-historical logic of alienation, competition and domination. The oppositional stance of all such struggles, vis-à-vis oppression and/or exploitation indicates that. We, who live and do politics in the shadow of Soviet collapse and the Chinese perversion, should always remember that such oppositional struggles are not meant to end in the triumph of labour over capital.

Labour does not dominate capital it becomes capital itself. Such working class movements, in spite of being posed and articulated in oppositional terms, must exude the awareness that they are part of a larger continuous struggle that constantly seeks to decimate both capitalism and the ontology of 'working people' within it. The struggle is actually about obliterating the difference between dominator and dominated, not the triumph of the latter over the former. Elias alludes to that implicit logic of revolutionary politics through *Khowabnama* when he depicts myths as dreams.

Tamijer Baap and Cherag Ali, by virtue of being members of the poor rural underclass of 1940s' East Bengal, are compelled to confront the oppressive existential reality with their 'dreamy' myths of rebellion and emancipation. Yet, in being posed as dreams, myths become as much a negation of the alienating logic of existential reality as the confrontational stance that such logic compels them to strike against that reality. In Elias, myths and their oppressed bearers confront existential reality and its oppressive purveyors not to defeat or dominate them, but to dissolve the boundaries that separate them and in the process transfigure their own existential ontology. Myth and reality, in his scheme, are related to each other, not through what appears to be a logic of absolute separation and opposition, but through a logic of inflection and perpetual process.

Such a historical relationship can, as we have seen above, also be conceived and represented as a 'synchronic' constellation of existential and possible (mythic) realities. Elias's 'structural' constellation of realities has the oppressive pre-Tebhaga existential reality of 1940s' East Bengal 'synchronically' integrated with the equally lived reality of the Tebhaga movement through a relationship of resistance against the former's logic of alienation and exploitation. The Tebhaga movement, in turn, is bound by the logic of anti-exploitative struggle with the 18th-19th century Sanyasi and Fakir rebellions, which in turn inflect the oppressive pre-Tebhaga existential reality as its inverted-critical knowledge in the form of myths. Those myths, especially in the critique they negatively pose to the alienating and exploitative logic of pre-Tebhaga Bengal, are integrated with the Tebhaga struggle as an alternative possible reality that the struggle seeks to accomplish. Elias constructs this kaleidoscopic world of infinite historical inflections in *Khowabnama* to allude to the possibility that this *fiction* on Tebhaga within his, and subsequently our, existential time of alienation is seen inflecting that lived reality as its critical-negative possibility. The fabulistic texture that Elias gives to slain militant Tamij, who with his bullet-riddled neck climbs into the moon, echoes the local myth of the dead Muslim ascetic, who after he had been killed by the East India Company had made his home on a local tree. His deliberate mythification of the reality of Tebhaga as depicted in his novel is supposed to negatively imply the possible reality of his *fiction* and thus open, not close, the dialectic. It's a possibility that waits to be actualised through collective political action. Much like Keramat and Tamij's rebellion actualised the reality immanent in the fables and dreams of their oppressed community.

Ghatak sees a beginning that has been lost and an end that cannot be reached. So, there is failure. For Elias, however, there is neither beginning nor end. There is only a never-ending journey with halting stations along the way. Success exists only in deferment and failure there is none. There is, however, only a small problem: we stop at one of those halting stations for far too long.

Note: The germ of the idea that is this essay is the result of a critical engagement with 'History's creative counterpart', a paper on Akhtaruzzaman Elias by critic Shubhoranjan Dasgupta.

BIBLIOGRAPHY

Adorno, Theodor W., *Aesthetic Theory*, tr. Robert Hullot-Kentor (Viva-Continuum, London, 2005)

Badiou, Alain, *Metapolitics* (from Jason Barker's introduction to it), tr. Jason Barker (Verso, London, 2006)

Balibar, Etienne, 'The Basic Concepts of Historical Materialism'. In *Reading Capital* by Louis Althusser and Etienne Balibar, tr. Ben Brewster (Verso, London, 1999)

Balibar, Etienne, 'The Elements of the Structure and their History'. In *Reading Capital* by Louis Althusser and Etienne Balibar, tr. Ben Brewster (Verso, London, 1999)

Benjamin, Walter, 'A Berlin Chronicle'. In *Reflections*, tr. Edmund Jephcott (Schocken Books, New York, 1986)

Benjamin, Walter, 'Surrealism'. In *Reflections*, tr. Edmund Jephcott (Schocken Books, New York, 1986)

Cassirer, Ernst, *Language and Myth*, tr. Susanne K. Langer (Dover Publications, New York, 1953)

Deluze, Giles, *Foucault*, tr. Sean Hand (Viva-Continuum, London, 2007)

Ghatak, Ritwik, 'Cinema and the Subjective Factor'. In *Rows and Rows of Fences* (Seagull Books, Calcutta, 2000)

Elias, Akhtaruzzaman, *Chilekotar Sepai* (The University Press Limited, Dhaka, 2000)

Elias, Akhtaruzzaman, *Khowabnama* (Naya Udyog, Kolkata)

Ilyenkov, Evald V., *The Dialectics of the Abstract and the Concrete in Marx's Capital*, tr. Sergei Syrovatkin (Aakar Books, New Delhi, 2008)

Jameson, Fredric, *Archaeologies of the Future* (Verso, London, 2007)

Zizek, Slavoj, *The Puppet And The Dwarf* (The MIT Press, Cambridge, Massachusetts, 2003)